THE MARVELOUS THREE CB&D

The Marvelous Three CB&D

Author and Illustrator
by
Kareem Caldwell

Copyright Page

© 2009

by Kareem Caldwell

Printed in the United States of America

ISBN:

978-0-578-10310-5

Published by Kareem Caldwell, N. Charleston, South

Carolina

Page Design and Composition: Kareem Caldwell, N.

Charelston, South Carolina

Library Of Congress Registration Number:

TXu 1-706-697

Once upon a time...

There was a farm owned by the Crowns.

It had animals everywhere and animals all around!

The animals soon added an

extra family to their family tree; it was a litter of kittens!

The mother of them all was named Lindy.

Sadly, Lindy was very sick and it was decided that

the kittens had to be sold.

The Crowns hoped for the best

for their kittens and their new homes.

But Lindy had one kitten that

she knew had a heart of gold.

Core was his name. She didn't want

him to be sold. He was such a blessing to the family that

Core was never sold. The mother kitten soon passed

away, but she left Core with something to

hold – a smile and a family.

Core was adventurous; he decided to leave the farm

to see the world.

Dore was a playful little pup;

he was friendly with everyone he saw.

He lived on his own and traveled by paw.

He knew how to survive, and he loved it all.

The families he met, he loved.

No matter the place, he got pets and hugs.

Each day, he spends time with the children,

and there's one he'll never forget:

Debra, a handicapped girl in a wheelchair.

She loved Dore for his warmth. She knew that he really cared.

For a while, Dore lived in a store owned by the Forts.

Dore became bored, so he left the store

to find new adventures.

He used his nose, like a dog always does.

He traveled and traveled down a long road,

looking for food for himself

so he could keep up with his health.

Bore was a bird from the park

He left his nest far away

and went to fetch worms for his friends.

As he took his time flying through the air,

clouds moved in, making him blind.

He finally *whooshed! P*ast the clouds;

he made it free.

Sadly, he didn't know where

he was, not even the bees so he continued to fly.

Time passed by, and his wings begin to ache.

While he rested on a wire, he spotted two animals.

They were not birds like himself.

He watched them from above, and then s*wooped* down to see

who they were. He hid and waited. Bore saw a cat and said, "A cat is coming. What should I do?"

He looked again and noticed that the other was a dog.

"A dog is coming, too! What should I do?" he said.

Core, the cat who came from the farm and Dore, the dog who

meant no harm bumped into each other and looked at one another.

Both said "Hi!" as Bore stared in surprise.

"Is it true? A cat and dog are communicating? Is it me, or am I going

crazy?" he said to himself. Bore decided to greet them.

He came out of hiding and said, "Hi." All three of them were very nice.

They talked and laughed; they explained to each other how they crossed

each other's paths. "I'm Core," the cat said. "I left my home to see the

world." "I'm Dore, the pup who is on a quest,

who lived with the Forts that own a store," said the dog.

"I'm Bore," said the bird.

"I was getting worms for my friends,

until I got lost in the clouds and the wind."

As they were talking, they all noticed that they were different.

Bore said, "I have wings and I can fly."

Core said, "I can meow and it sounds like a cry."

Dore said, "I like to bark, and I love trees and parks.

by the way, we are in a park.

Let's venture around and see what there is to see."

They grinned with joy and, although they were different,

they all got along with each other. They all said at the same time,

"I have a feeling that we're going to become like brothers!"

As they walked through the park and enjoyed each other's company,

a stomach growled, and then another, and then there was another

stomach that growled. The three of them said, "BOY, AM I HUNGRY!"

Bore said, "I would like a nice juicy worm so that my stomach won't

churn." Core said, "I would like a saucer of milk that would help."

Dore groaned, "My tummy needs a bone." "Hey, I know a spot where we

can chow." he said. "I can fly." Bore replied. "Where?" Core said with an

eager eye. "Follow your nose, that's my rule," Dore said. He soon found a

bone just for him, and then he sniffed again.

"Over there!" he said with a grin. "I smell worms, you can dig for them."

Bore flew like a jet to catch the worms.

"I smell milk coming from around the corner." Dore said to Core. "I

found it!" Core said as he spotted milk by the door.

They raced through the park, "Who's going to get there first?" Bore yelled

with excitement. Core said, "Me!"

Dore said, "No, me! I'm the fastest - watch and see!"

And so they raced.

They all had their meals, and enjoyed each other's company.

Bore ate his worm and said, "My worm was delicious."

Core said, "And so was my milk."

Core asked Dore. "How is your bone?"

Dore did not answer, until finally he

swallowed and replied,

"I don't talk with my mouth full; that is rude.

But it was very, very, very, delicious."

After they finished their meals,

all of a sudden, sleepiness fell upon them.

Bore said, "I need to rest my little wings."

Core said, "I wish I could lie around a warm, cozy fire."

Bore said, "That sounds good."

They all left to find shelter and saw light spilling out from a

door. Once they entered through the door,

Dore said, "This place doesn't look so bad."

They followed Dore into a room where there was warmth and a cozy

bed and a TV. "Welcome to my home! For now!"

Dore shouted, and they all laughed.

They headed to a room where an old TV was still working,

and they all sat to view the show before it was time to go to sleep.

Dore said, "Oh, boy! Dinner *and* a movie!"

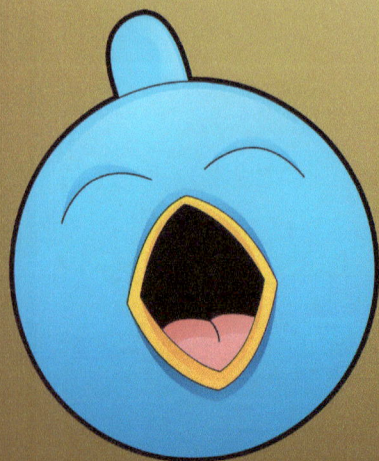

Y
A
W
N

Soon, their mouths opened wide and their eyes closed tight.

Sleepy time was upon them, and they were ready to say good night.

"You can sleep here, you guys." Dore pointed across the room.

There was a set of beds made just for animals that have no place to stay.

The show was finally over, and the night had ended.

The three little friends were ready to tuck themselves in.

They again began to yawn.

Bore, Core and Dore placed their paws

and feathers over their mouths;

Bore chirped, Core meowed, and Dore barked,

as they all showed signs of comfort. They all said good night.

The day had ended and the night was upon them.

They slept in their beds dreaming about the next day

of adventure, fun and play.

Three little animals, different in all ways, had become best friends.

No one fought, and no one cared,

they all had something special to share. Friendship.

Now it's time for bed and time to sleep.

The adventures of Bore, Core, and Dore will begin again with a

new day full of fun and excitement! As new friends.

THE END

<u>ABOUT THE AUTHOR</u>

I was born 1lb and 14oz with a 10% chance of living. My mother, Mildred Anderson-Taylor has seen it all with her own two eyes as I developed into a young man. During my childhood, it was very difficult for me to grasp and adapt to learning. My mother worked with me diligently to get to where I am now. The doctor's said to my mother, "That your son will be mentally challenged," and that she would have to take care of me for the rest of her life. Boy were they wrong...I went to an art magnet program for three years in middle school in Miami, Florida and then high school and then college in Orlando, Florida; a very prominent institute which helped develop my writing skills and drawing abilities. While I was in school, I had an idea because of my childhood to devote my life to writing children's books of encouragement and adventure. My main interest is to stimulate children's minds on all levels to be very visual and tactile to be hands on because it's a learning process throughout life. This is my passion and dedication to all children of all denominations. Also, I would like to thank everyone for supporting me in this endeavor, there are so many names that can not be named, thank you.

3Things

COMING SOON

www.ingramcontent.com/pod-product-compliance
Lightning Source LLC
Chambersburg PA
CBHW041810040426
42449CB00001B/48

9 780578 103105